Window, Harrison County (201-01)

Lingering Spirit

A photographic tribute to Indiana's fading, forlorn, and forgotten places

John Bower
foreword by Judy O'Bannon

STUDIO INDIANA

D1526498

Published by:

Studio Indiana
430 N. Sewell Road
Bloomington, IN 47408

©2003

Publisher's Cataloging-in-Publication Data
Bower, John.
      Lingering Spirit: a photographic tribute to Indiana's fading, forlorn, and forgotten
places / by John Bower; foreword by Judy O'Bannon; essay by Lynn Marie Bower.

        p.   cm.
      ISBN 0-9745186-0-3
      1. Photography, Artistic.   2. Indiana—Pictorial works.   3. Indiana—Description
and travel—Views.   I. Bower, John, 1949-.   II. Title.
      TR647.B69   2003
      779.944   CIP 2003096389

INDIANA ARTS COMMISSION

Connecting people to the arts

This activity is made possible in part by the Indiana
Arts Commission, a state agency, with funds from
the Indiana General Assembly and the National
Endowment for the Arts

Foreword

A haunting and yet an encouraging journey awaits you as you engage in an exploration of the soul of a people, found in the photographs of the objects they've left behind. In *Lingering Spirit*, John Bower has stripped away the overgrowth that accumulates and hides from us the remaining skeleton of a previous time and place. Through his eye, we feel the message not just of those who went before us, but our own inner wailings of today and hopefully our resolve for tomorrow.

I often ask myself why I drag home abandoned pieces of rusty metal, old worn wooden broken parts, and fragments of pottery and glass. Why do I long to touch and see and even heal remnants of the workings of yesterday? Why do I like "old stuff?" It is because people have rubbed against them as they did their dance with life and left their marks. For me, it's an intimate experience that evokes the very spirit of people who've walked this path before me. As I feel the objects with my hands and see them with my eyes, their spirit connects with mine. I sense my belonging in the ongoing web of the community of life. And, for the moments of wonder and for the acts of neglect, we are all there together.

The photographs in *Lingering Spirit* speak to us as a beacon, urging us to experience the essence of the human journey. This is a book of our story. The story of each of our every days that grow to form the shape of our destiny. Through the images of old cars, worn barns and abandoned homes, John Bower introduces us to ourselves.

Just as I'm sure there is always a new use, a real value, an unrealized potential in old weathered objects, I'm given confidence that there is a future of promise for all of us.

Judy O'Bannon
First Lady of Indiana
August 2003

Store, Brown County (136-05)

Preface

This book project didn't start out as a project at all. Instead, it evolved—rather slowly—as a result of taking rides in the country. Throughout our marriage, my wife, Lynn, and I have spent much of our leisure time driving on back roads in various parts of the Midwest. For us, discovering something interesting and unforeseen around the next bend has provided a great deal of enjoyment. During many of our early years together, I didn't take a camera with me. Then, one day, I simply decided to put my camera in the car whenever we left home. So, we'd head off for an afternoon drive, see a picturesque scene or building, and I'd stop to photograph it. For a long time, both the driving and the photography were quite random.

After a while, I found that I was photographing more and more machinery, buildings, vehicles, and man-made structures that were decaying, worn-out, or abandoned—objects that were once the pride of their owners and their age, but were now well past their prime. Upon seeing some of these images for the first time, a friend asked "Why are you taking so many pictures of things that are falling apart?"

At first, I couldn't answer her question. But I soon understood that I was recording on film more than the visible, physicality where lives had been lived. I was being drawn to the energy of the individuals whose lives had once been intertwined with the buildings and other objects. So, for me, there are people in these images—it's just that they can no longer be seen.

As a result, I believe my photographs are more than simple snapshots. They are memorials, tributes, and monuments to the lives of the people who moved on—the homeowners, equipment operators, builders, employers, employees, families—those who have left some of themselves in the remains of their now-cast-aside possessions. I often wonder about these people. What happened to the women who raised their families, canned vegetables, and sewed quilts in that now-empty farm house? What about the men who worked in that dilapidated factory? Who was the original owner of that rusted-out pickup truck? What happened to the masons who built that one-room schoolhouse, and the children who sat at its desks? I know I could talk to neighbors, track down relatives, research old newspaper clippings, or visit historical societies, and get some of the answers. But, without a doubt, those answers would be incomplete. They couldn't possibly tell the entire story or, perhaps, even the most important story.

So, without knowing the specific details of a place, I record what I see and what I feel. Some of my subjects are historically or architecturally significant, others are quite ordinary. Some evoke a warm sense of nostalgia, some are stark and sad. But my subjects were all central, vital, and dynamic to someone. They are a record of the spirit that has been left behind. In fact, they are a record of the true history of South-Central Indiana—the history of the day-to-day lives of ordinary people.

The Roman poet Ovid said time was "the devourer of all things." Even though our contemporary buildings and machines will also eventually turn to dust, I can't imagine them ever having the dignity of a forlorn country church with no congregation, or a battered and rusted tractor no longer able to plow. To me, that which was built many decades ago often retains a presence, a vitality—a spirit—that's rarely found in today's complex, plastic-infested society. It's this soulful, aging, built environment I am compelled to record on film—before it's completely devoured by time. Actually, some of my subjects are already gone. In some cases they were razed and hauled away the day after I shot them.

On one of our many rides in the country, Lynn and I casually discussed the possibility of assembling my photographs into a book. Even though the idea remained somewhat nebulous, we started going for drives with the specific purpose of taking pictures. Over time, as the project started to gel, then solidify, a title became apparent, and we decided to definitely publish a book. But in order to keep it to a manageable size, we would limit it to photos taken in ten specific counties in South-Central Indiana—Bartholomew, Brown, Crawford, Harrison, Jackson, Lawrence, Monroe, Orange, Perry, and Washington (see the map on page 141). While all the photos on these pages were taken in these particular counties, my subjects are often so typically Midwestern that many are reminiscent of locales in Indiana's other 82 counties.

Once we had a definite goal in mind, I obtained maps for each of my chosen ten counties, and Lynn and I started marking off the roads we covered. Eventually, when the weather was agreeable, we drove 90% of the paved roads, unpaved roads, and dead-end roads on my maps—almost 15,000 miles—seeking "fading, forlorn, and forgotten places" to photograph. All the images in this book were taken over a three-and-a-half-year period between 2000 and 2003.

About midway through the project, I applied for an Individual Artist Grant from the Indiana Arts Commission to help publish my book. After their jurying process was complete, I was pleased to be awarded a $1,000 grant—not nearly enough to actually pay for publication costs, but a nice check nonetheless. I thank them very much for their support. I'd also like to thank Judy O'Bannon for writing such a heartfelt Foreword, and Lynn, my wife, lover, and best friend, who is responsible for the actual design of the book, who wrote the essay on South-Central Indiana, and who is my most-valued critic.

For many years I used a Minolta 35-mm camera of average quality, but for this project I purchased a Mamiya 645 medium-format camera. This camera produces negatives that are

60 mm x 45 mm—somewhat larger than a 35-mm camera's 35 mm x 24 mm negatives—so it yields sharper enlargements. When photographing buildings I often use a shift lens (also called a perspective-control lens), which can be adjusted to remove any vertical distortion (keystoning) caused by perspective. I almost always use a tripod.

I tend to use Ilford FP-4+ film, but have also used Kodak T-Max (100 speed) film, and I process the film myself in a conventional wet darkroom that I installed in our home. I also do my own printing—on Ilford Multigrade RC paper—and generally treat my prints with a sulfide toner. Toning helps preserve the prints, and it produces a slight sepia (brownish) coloration which I believe is in keeping with the subject matter.

I'm often asked why I don't use a digital camera and an ink-jet printer. The answer is that I have nothing against digital photography, I simply prefer using conventional film and working in a darkroom. Similarly, I have nothing against color film, it's just that I prefer black-and-white. Showing less (black, white, and tones of gray, rather than a rainbow of thousands of colors) helps me get to the essence of my subjects.

Over the course of photographing the counties of South-Central Indiana, I shot nearly two hundred rolls of film. Together, Lynn (an accomplished artist) and I had a difficult time selecting the specific photographs for these pages because there were just so many compelling images to choose from. In laying out the book, I decided on an organization starting with homes, then buildings associated with livelihood, followed by means of transportation, and finally ending with images reflecting the larger community.

I've purposely not listed specific locations for my photographs—for several reasons. First of all, many of my subjects are on private property, and I don't want to encourage trespassing. Also, I quickly learned that the road names shown on signs (when there were signs) were sometimes different from the road names on my maps, so I probably couldn't give an accurate location if I wanted to. And, finally, Lynn and I found it most enjoyable to serendipitiously discover interesting places on our own, accidentally, without any inkling of what would be around the next curve in the road. So, we'd like to encourage others to take a destinationless, meandering drive through Southern Indiana to see where it leads them.

John Bower

House, Bartholomew County (150-14)

When I looked up the word *house* in my dictionary, the definition read "a place where people live." But my experience tells me a house is much more than that. Because I remember something special about each of the 18 houses I've lived in, I feel that a part of me still clings to those buildings, and always will. So, when I see an abandoned, dilapidated house, I know it is filled with memories. If I decide to stop and take some pictures, I first look for interesting details like gingerbread, wainscoting, or door hardware. I'll also take notice of a particular layout of windows, discarded furniture, or how the building relates to its environment. Then, as I look around, I start to sense the pride of the carpenters and masons who built the place. I sometimes even pick up on this in small, two-room shacks built with unskilled hands. And it doesn't take long before I start wondering about the people who lived there—who hoped, dreamed, loved, laughed, cried, prayed, and grieved. It's this accumulated emotional residue that appeals to me as much as the structure itself.

Dining-room table, Monroe County (084-06)

Interior door, Washington County (237-06)

House, Orange County (173-13)

Living room, Harrison County (173-11)

House, Crawford County (170-03)

Rear porch, Perry County (166-04)

Front porch, Orange County (161-04)

14

House, Bartholomew County (184-08)

Window, Washington County (237-05)

Window, Crawford County (226-02)

Window sill, Perry County (111-11)

Window, Washington County (237-14)

House interior, Bartholomew County (178-15)

House, Lawrence County (160-01)

House with sewing machine in window, Jackson County (186-11)

House, Orange County (239-10)

Entry door, Harrison County (197-11)

Entry doors, Lawrence County (220-11)

Entry door, Lawrence County (155-07)

Entry door, Crawford County (196-06)

Entry doors, Monroe County (129-05)

22

Cabinet, Crawford County (225-08)

Kitchen sink, Perry County (113-04)

Bed, Brown County (136-12)

Clothes closet, Jackson County (187-15)

Kitchen range, Jackson County (141-03)

House, Crawford County (195-03)

House, Orange County (161-09)

House, Lawrence County (159-03)

Stairway, Harrison County (200-09)

Interior door, Bartholomew County (062-09)

28

Entry door, Crawford County (228-15)

Entry door, Harrison County (199-11)

Entry door, Harrison County (198-02)

Entry door, Jackson County (232-05)

Entry door, Brown County (131-14)

30

Back porch, Perry County (168-15)

House, Bartholomew County (077-10)

House, Orange County (204-11)

Kitchen, Crawford County (224-01)

Kitchen with wheelchair, Harrison County (200-13)

Kitchen, Brown County (133-04)

Canning jars, Jackson County (232-10)

Trunk, Washington County (236-10)

Fireplace, Perry County (206-03)

Washing machine, Perry County (216-12)

Chair, Crawford County (224-08)

House, Bartholomew County (162-04)

Entry door with typewriter, Orange County (190-07)

Fireplace, Crawford County (224-10)

House, Perry County (216-05)

House, Lawrence County (158-04)

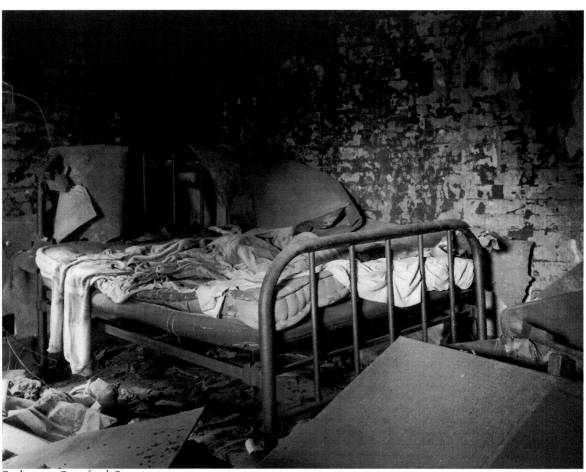

Bedroom, Crawford County (224-04)

Bedroom, Harrison County (170-13)

Bedroom, Lawrence County (143-07)

42

House, Washington County (210-03)

House, Orange County (203-09)

Washing machine, Lawrence County (156-12)

House, Harrison County (219-12)

House, Harrison County (199-13)

44

Log house, Lawrence County (155-05)

House, Harrison County (199-08)

Cistern, Orange County (160-07)

Log corner with horseshoe, Brown County (140-13)

School teacher's log house, Perry County (165-11)

Porch with piano, Lawrence County (149-01)

Refrigerator, Washington County (192-15)

Washing machine, Bartholomew County (153-09)

Kitchen shelves, Lawrence County (220-09)

Front-porch chair, Brown County (131-15)

Stairway, Harrison County (107-11)

51

Wash tubs, Lawrence County (158-05)

Barn, Brown County (214-10)

The way old barns were built has always intrigued me. Their oversized, hand-hewn timbers, mortised-and-tenoned, then pegged in place, were carefully crafted one at a time, then assembled during a barn raising by friends and neighbors or, perhaps, by a crew specializing in erecting large buildings. I'm also drawn to the varied shapes of hand-made corn cribs and small outbuildings. To my eye and sense of design, some of them border on sculpture, with a pleasing balance of space, materials, form, and function. Often, when I look at these utilitarian buildings, I can sense the confidence of the builders who crafted them, and the satisfaction of the farmers who used them. Many were built to last—not just for 25 years, like today's pole buildings, but for generations. And last they do, for long after their useful life has expired, they still stand, partially collapsed, riddled by termites—yet possessing a quiet, well-worn dignity.

Barn, Jackson County (098-02)

54

Barn, Jackson County (246-04)

Barn, Monroe County (069-03)

Barn ladder, Monroe County (069-04)

Barn, Bartholomew County (162-08)

Barn, Orange County (202-13)

Well house for orchard, Lawrence County (149-09)

58

Windmill, Bartholomew County (162-03)

Distant barn, Monroe County (079-03)

Tractors, Orange County (190-08)

Tractor, Brown County (132-13)

Tractor, Orange County (190-01)

Chicken coop, Washington County (238-08)

Farm building, Harrison County (213-05)

64

Tractor, Harrison County (171-15)

Barn, Crawford County (167-03)

Barn, Washington County (210-04)

Barn, Brown County (132-08)

Barn with mailbox, Bartholomew County (178-08)

Farm building, Lawrence County (148-13)

Corn crib, Harrison County (212-05)

Silo, Bartholomew County (179-12)

Corn cribs, Bartholomew County (049-12)

Barn, Bartholomew County (162-10)

Barn, Brown County (213-12)

Farm wagon, Harrison County (212-10)

72

Barn, Monroe County (231-01)

Barn, Perry County (206-10)

Foundation corner, Brown County (140-11)

Basketball hoop, Washington County (209-05)

Barn door, Orange County (240-02)

Barn, Jackson County (182-02)

Thrashing machine, Washington County (209-03)

Tractor wheel, Washington County (211-02)

Barn interior, Perry County (163-09)

Shed, Washington County (191-14)

Barn interior, Brown County (076-10)

Barn foundation, Monroe County (117-05)

Barn door, Lawrence County (144-12)

Outbuilding, Lawrence County (155-01)

Barn door, Monroe County (117-03)

Barn with cows, Jackson County (141-07)

Barn doors, Harrison County (219-02)

Automobiles, Lawrence County (149-05)

Sometimes, when I spot a car or pickup truck sitting on flat tires, slowly rusting away, I picture a little boy riding home from the dealership with his daddy when its paint and chrome were shiny. Perhaps, later, when the newness had worn off, his older brother borrowed it for a date with a special girlfriend. That car or truck made routine trips to town for groceries, to church, to visit relatives, and to the funerals of friends. We all have many such memories, so it's no wonder some people simply can't part with their vehicles when they no longer run. Instead, they park them, in fields, along fence rows, or in overgrown woodlots, where they serve as memorials to the past. Many of us also have a special relationship with railroads. I recall my first train ride when I was five years old, placing pennies on the tracks after school to be flattened, the times I was in a hurry to get somewhere and was stopped at a crossing by 100 boxcars rumbling by. But when railroads outlived their usefulness, the track, engines, and cars usually ended up in scrap heaps. That's why I smile when I come across an abandoned train station, a lonely bridge without rails, or a retired passenger car that has, against the odds, survived.

Automobile, Crawford County (196-03)

Gasoline pump (29.9¢ per gallon), Harrison County (197-05)

Truck interior, Washington County (237-03)

Automobile, Lawrence County (159-15)

Tow truck, Washington County (192-07)

Automobile, Washington County (192-02)

Fire truck, Brown County (058-01)

Truck, Jackson County (233-07)

Automobile, Brown County (138-11)

Automobile, Washington County (209-15)

Automobile, Crawford County (228-13)

Automobile window, Lawrence County (156-08)

Truck, Washington County (209-14)

Truck, Jackson County (080-11)

Automobile, Monroe County (110-13)

Fire-engine siren, Jackson County (182-06)

92

Covered bridge, Jackson County (234-11)

Railroad-bridge piers, Monroe County (067-12)

Railroad bridge, Monroe County (221-15)

Railroad tunnel and semaphore, Lawrence County (145-08)

Railroad bridge, Bartholomew County (188-08)

Railroad station, Jackson County (242-01)

Trolley car, Brown County (147-10)

Railroad passenger cars, Orange County (130-05)

Railroad steam engine, Orange County (130-06)

Railroad passenger car interior, Orange County (123-13)

Stores, Crawford County (167-13)

As Lynn and I drove around South-Central Indiana, it was refreshing to discover a small town with a thriving country store. As in the past, they were generally mom-and-pop operations. But the range of merchandise has evolved—from the dry goods, hardware, and penny candy of yesterday, to packaged snacks, pizza, and video rentals. Of course, over the decades, many of these stores have disappeared without a trace. But for every one still in operation, we found another that had long been out-of-business, and was slowly falling apart. Even though there wasn't a soul around these old places, as I set up my camera, I could almost hear the latest news that had once been dispensed around the wood stove, or under the roof of the front porch. Back then, this talk was as vital a commodity as sugar. We also came across a variety of other abandoned businesses. I particularly liked the brick kilns and limestone mills because I've always had an interest in how things are made. These buildings speak not of gossip, but of hard work, sore muscles, and drudgery—and also a deep sense of accomplishment.

Doctor's office, Orange County (204-04)

Store, Harrison County (198-05)

Side of store, Washington County (107-06)

Roadside eatery, Harrison County (197-09)

Tourist cabins, Crawford County (169-10)

Store, Brown County (214-04)

Store, Perry County (166-08)

Store, Jackson County (180-11)

Store, Crawford County (226-05)

Soda-pop machine, Crawford County (225-15)

Store, Harrison County (198-11)

Brick-making kilns, Jackson County (181-08)

Factory stove, Jackson County (074-07)

Empire State Building quarry, Lawrence County (238-10)

Limestone mill, Monroe County (101-09)

Limestone quarry, Monroe County (241-12)

112

Limestone mill, Monroe County (128-13)

Excavator bucket, Perry County (217-10)

Incinerator, Lawrence County (063-08)

Concrete-block plant, Monroe County (063-15)

Machinery, Monroe County (110-07)

Toledo scales, Harrison County (199-12)

Sawmill, Monroe County (231-07)

Factory stairway, Monroe County (161-15)

Gristmill water wheel, Washington County (208-04)

School bus, Jackson County (186-01)

As you might expect, you never see as many forsaken community buildings as abandoned houses and barns. In the case of churches, when a congregation moved into a larger structure, the old building was usually taken over by another denomination eager for a home of their own. Many of the old one- and two-room schools have been turned into residences, or they're used for storage or as barns. With only a few being empty and in disrepair, I'm glad most of these buildings have been given a second life. It also pleases me to discover a particularly moving limestone grave marker. To me cemeteries aren't morbid, they're places filled with love. Every stone was erected in someone's memory, and many of those memories were happy ones. So, when I touch a hand-carved statue of a little girl, I don't dwell on the fact that she died young. Instead, I feel the immense joy she must have brought to her parents for them to commission a journeymen stone carver to create such a heartfelt memorial—a memorial that boldly proclaims "Remember!"

School, Harrison County (199-10)

120

School interior with books, Lawrence County (157-13)

School, Lawrence County (158-02)

School, Washington County (210-14)

School, Perry County (165-09)

School, Bartholomew County (154-09)

School, Jackson County (184-01)

School, Jackson County (184-02)

School–after the fire, Harrison County (211-14)

124

Court House (1821–1846), Crawford County (167-10)

Fire escape–County Home, Orange County (240-09)

Church, Harrison County (171-03)

Church interior, Perry County (215-12)

Church steeple, Monroe County (067-08)

Church, Crawford County (196-10)

130

Church basement, Monroe County (067-04)

Church camp, Lawrence County (177-06)

Cemetery, Washington County (176-08)

Cemetery fence, Bartholomew County (227-11)

Cemetery, Jackson County (183-06)

Cemetery statue, Lawrence County (118-15)

Cemetery statue, Harrison County (229-08)

Cemetery statue, Lawrence County (117-13)

Cemetery statue, Monroe County (071-14)

Cemetery statue, Washington County (246-15)

Pet cemetery marker, Monroe County (042-07)

Cemetery statue, Lawrence County (243-04)

Cemetery, Crawford County (166-13)

John Bower

I've always felt that knowing something about an artist will lead to a better understanding of his work. So, I include the following to shed some light on why I photograph the things I do.

For my first seven years, I lived in the northwest Indiana town of Fowler, where I remember having fun dismantling my toys (and occasionally putting them back together in different ways). The rest of my youth was spent in nearby Lafayette, where I was regularly involved with building projects. I particularly liked nailing together tree houses and hideouts in the woods behind our home because they provided a refuge from my five sisters. Because we lived at the bottom of two fairly long hills, I also put together a number of pushcarts. Then, by the time I reached high-school age, I progressed to crafting motorized mini-bikes and, eventually, a hot rod.

Because I've always had strong mechanical inclinations, and I lived near Purdue University, when it was time for college, I enrolled in Purdue's School of Engineering. However, the courses were too theoretical for my liking and midway through my freshman year I switched to an Industrial Education program. I really didn't want to be a shop teacher, which is what the curriculum prepared one for, but I enjoyed the coursework immensely. In fact, I thrived on the hands-on nature of woodworking, power mechanics, metalworking, etc. I particularly liked several graphic arts courses, where I picked up valuable information that would eventually help me publish a number of books. After graduating from Purdue, I accepted a Graduate Assistantship at Ball State University, and obtained my Masters degree. While in college, I took two of my electives in the Art Department, but never considered a switch to that major because I didn't think of myself as artistic. I considered myself more practical than an artist.

When it came time to enter the "real world," I accepted an Industrial-Arts teaching position at the Kendallville Middle school in the northeast corner of Indiana. It was there that I met my future wife, Lynn, who was the new Crafts teacher, and also in the Industrial-Arts department. We got married over Thanksgiving break of that year and honeymooned in South-Central Indiana—at the French Lick Springs Resort. We spent several days driving around the surrounding countryside, thoroughly enjoying the winding roads, hardwood forests, rolling hills, and quiet small towns. We thought about how nice it would be to live in the area, but it took over a decade before destiny finally allowed us to relocate in rural Monroe County.

Over the years, I've held jobs as a factory worker, draftsman, display designer, carpenter, and environmental engineer. I've also built and restored furniture, my wife and I have completely remodeled two houses, and I've constructed several houses from scratch. While I now use some power tools, I started out using hand tools, and I learned to appreciate the heft of a hammer, the sharp edge of a chisel, the smooth corners on a piece of steel left by a file. I've also written technical books dealing with healthy-house construction—houses designed and built to have good indoor air quality. My experiences have made me respectful of craftsmen of all sorts—carpenters, upholsterers, cabinetmakers, masons, machinists, etc.

As the years passed, and I became seriously interested in photography, it began to dawn on me that I had some artist in me after all. And, for me, photography has turned out to be the perfect medium, being a synthesis of the mechanical (f-stops, depth of field, film processing) and the intangible (composition, mood, emotion). I particularly enjoy photographing things that have been built with human hands. So, when I find a rusting farm truck, a dilapidated one-room school, or a sagging barn, I'm drawn to it. And, if I know it may not be there in a few years (or even a few days), I feel compelled to capture it on film.

John Bower

To learn more about John Bower and Studio Indiana,
or to purchase John's photographs, please visit
www.studioindiana.com

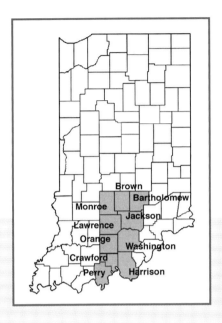

South-Central Indiana

The ten counties chosen for this project constitute the very heart of Southern Indiana. The area is filled with beautiful, undulating terrain—the southern hills. The extent and degree of hilliness varies greatly from place to place, with some areas gently rolling, while other places are rugged, with rough knobs and deep ravines.

Much of South-Central Indiana is forested with hardwoods such as maple, tulip poplar, beech, and oak. But pines, cedars and other softwood species can be found as well. Flowering deciduous trees, including white dogwood, redbud, and persimmon, are beautiful in springtime. Deer, turkeys, hawks, woodpeckers, songbirds, squirrels, ground hogs, snakes, opossums, raccoons, vultures, foxes, and bats abound in much of the area.

Beginning in the 1930s, hundreds of acres have been incorporated into the Hoosier National Forest, a number of state forests, state recreational areas, and state parks (Brown County and Spring Mill). The area is crisscrossed with hiking trails—including the Knobstone Trail, which has been favorably compared with the better-known Appalachian Trail.

Many of the townships contain vast areas of cropland and meadows, especially where the terrain is relatively flat. Others have smaller pockets of agricultural land, often in river and stream valleys. Popular crops include corn, soybeans, wheat, and hay, but fields of tomatoes, melons, pumpkins, and tobacco are not uncommon. In places, fruit orchards of peaches and apples are cultivated. Inside fenced grasslands, herds of beef cattle and, less commonly, dairy cows, graze. Also seen are horses, mules, donkeys, sheep, and hogs, as well as a few exotics such as llamas, ostriches, and elk. Long pole buildings devoted to raising poultry have been erected in a number of places.

Under much of South-Central Indiana lies limestone. In some areas, outcroppings are exposed to the surface, in other places it is hidden beneath the topsoil. Exceptionally high-grade architectural limestone is quarried in Monroe and Lawrence Counties where piles of colossal blocks of roughly cut stone are heaped near pits of deep blue water. Nearby, you can sometimes find a hulking shed constructed of wood, iron, or steel with windows containing hundreds of small glass panes. Here, workers would mill the raw stone, and artisans would carve decorative building adornments and statuary. While some operations have been abandoned, others remain busy. At other sites, limestone of lesser quality is crushed into gravel, for use on roads, or in making concrete. Brown sandstone is also quarried in places and clay (once used in local brick manufactories) is common. Occasionally, oil wells can be seen—some are pumping while others are dormant and capped.

Abundant water is another key feature of the region, with rivers including the East Fork of the White River and the Ohio River—Indiana's southern boundary, which is plied by multiple, linked barges, often loaded with coal. The Lost River is probably the most unusual in the region. Through various "sinks," it disappears below ground, then reappears on the surface through "rises." Another important stream, the Blue River, is popular with canoeists. While there are few natural lakes, there are many man-made ones, including small private ponds, and large reservoirs—the largest being Monroe and Patoka Lakes, both of which are surrounded by natural areas and public-access points. The Muscatatuck National Wildlife Refuge (Jackson County) was created as a welcome rest area for migrating waterfowl.

Historically, sulfur-rich springs and creeks have been important. Because these foul-smelling waters were once considered healthful, they gave birth to spas and hotels such as the French Lick Springs Resort and the West Baden Springs Hotel, both in Orange County. Built and rebuilt over many decades, these two landmarks had their glory years in the decades prior to the Great Depression, but remain popular tourist destinations.

Other natural features include caves. Some privately owned ones are accessible only by formal permission to trained spelunkers, but others are open to the public, including Squire Boone Caverns in Harrison County, Marengo and Wyandotte in Crawford County, and Bluespring Caverns in Lawrence County. In northeast Monroe County, large underground caverns are used as storage areas for natural gas. Widespread karst geologic areas often have sinkholes—small to large depressions in the ground where rain water collects and seeps underground through the soil and limestone.

For thousands of years, Indiana was literally what its name means—land of the Indians. Then, in 1679, the French explorer La Salle became one of the first Europeans to visit this part of the continent, hoping to bolster France's military power and commercial dominance of the area. In time, small trading posts were established, including those at French Lick (Orange County) and Vallonia (Jackson County), where highly-prized beaver and other animal pelts were exchanged by native peoples for manufactured goods.

Once the Treaty of Paris was signed in 1763 (concluding the French and Indian War), France ceded all it's lucrative North American holdings east of the Mississippi River to Great Britain. However, after the American Revolution, a defeated Britain was obliged to relinquish her own claims. Soon after, the Continental Congress passed the Ordinance of 1787 to create the Northwest Territory. With the advent of official land surveys and sales, American settlers poured into the area. By 1800, the Indiana Territory was carved out. It consisted of what is now Indiana, Illinois, Wisconsin, and Michigan, and part of Minnesota. Finally, statehood for Indiana was granted in 1816, with the boundaries we all recognize today.

Unfortunately, war, disease, persuasion (sometimes friendly, sometimes forceful), treaty, and land purchase, steadily pushed the Native American populations (mostly Algonquin-speaking Woodland tribes) out of Indiana. Over time, active measures were sanctioned to assure that Indian depopulation continued. In a relatively short time, the "land of the Indians" became a place with very few remaining.

The white pioneers who replaced the Indians were usually of English, Scot-Irish, Welsh, or German descent. Most traveled north from Virginia, the Carolinas, and Kentucky, but others arrived from New England. No matter their origin, the majority took up farming, while lesser numbers chose to be clergymen, shop keepers, millers, and tradesmen. An important motivation for some to move here (particularly for Quakers), was the illegality of slavery.

Because early settlers tended to be from the South, Indiana's first capitol was located at Corydon (Harrison County), not far from the Ohio River. Then, as the population rapidly expanded into the upper two-thirds of the state, the capital was moved northward to Indianapolis in 1825. Soon, the hill country of South-Central Indiana began losing the significant political influence and economic position it had once held.

Today, the ten counties of South-Central Indiana are, generally, less populated and less developed than other parts of the state, and personal incomes tend to be lower. In some areas, the population has so significantly shrunk that the land, so laboriously cleared by the original white settlers, has been abandoned, and is quickly being reclaimed by seedlings. The architectural limestone industry has also declined, but it still remains important to the economy of the region. Various other manufacturing facilities have also come and gone. However, each county has its share of new industries, with the largest industrial sectors being found in Columbus (Bartholomew County) and Bloomington (Monroe County).

The people who call this ten-county area home today are primarily white, including a sizable Amish community thriving in Lawrence and Orange Counties. Blacks are represented, with a few being descended from former slaves who originally came north via the underground railroad. (Leavenworth in Crawford County was one of the better-known stations on the route.) Although still relatively small, the Hispanic population is expected to grow considerably in the years ahead. The more populated counties (Bartholomew and Monroe) have citizens from every part of the globe due to their larger industrial base and, in the case of Monroe County, Indiana University.

With its casual, inviting atmosphere, South-Central Indiana is well known for its warm and friendly Hoosier Hospitality. Each of the ten counties actively promotes tourism—extolling the scenery, unique attractions, and amenities of which each is rightly proud. Of particular note is Nashville (Brown County), which has been an artist's colony for over a century. Its quaint downtown is filled with charming shops, galleries, and restaurants. In addition, historical and art museums offer outstanding exhibits, and the architectural tour of Columbus (Bartholomew County) offers visitors a view of buildings designed by some of the world's top architects. Many communities also host festivals throughout the warm-weather season.

Of course, not to be underestimated is the pleasure of simply driving around the hills and hollows of the ten counties that make up the heart of Southern Indiana—during any time of the year. On these back-county roads, you can meet interesting people, see unexpected sights, and learn more about our Hoosier heritage.

Lynn Marie Bower

Observatory–lower level, Monroe County (090-13) Observatory–upper level, Monroe County (091-02)

About a decade after this squatty, domed building first caught my attention, I finally got the urge to stop and investigate. When I walked through the tangled thicket of small trees and weeds taking over the property, I was amazed to see it was not a silo, as I'd thought, but an abandoned observatory. The door was wide open, and the stairs leading to the viewing platform were sturdy, so I climbed up to the second level. Of course, the telescope that once scanned the heavens was long gone, but I could clearly see how the entire dome was made to rotate atop the circular masonry wall, allowing the telescope to point in any direction. As I walked around taking pictures, I realized that this was a place devoted to capturing light, that it's purpose was to reveal objects we don't ordinarily see. And that is exactly what I had been doing. For months, as Lynn and I drove up and down Indiana's back roads, I had used my camera to capture the light from objects that most of us don't even notice, so I could make them visible—on the pages of this book. But there were other analogies as well: the observatory was a place devoted to searching and exploring, and Lynn and I had certainly explored many hundreds of square miles of territory. I also thought about how, when we see a star or galaxy, we are actually looking into its distant past, because it takes scores of years for its light to reach the earth. And that is my hope for *Lingering Spirit*—that it will provide a means of seeing and experiencing the energy of an earlier time, and will illuminate that which has gone before.

—JB